I Kept House In A Jungle

Anne Rainey Langley

I KEPT HOUSE IN A JUNGLE

The Spell of Primeval Tropics in Venezuela, Riotous With Strange Plants, Animals, and Snakes, Enthralls a Young American Woman

By Anne Rainey Langley

IN AN expanse of steaming jungle, which stretches savagely devoid of habitation to the Caribbean, Quiriquire sprawls like a large spider in the northeast of Venezuela. The small clearing in the matted tropical growth, 250 miles east of modern and sophisticated Caracas, occupies less than a square mile. Within this space is a self-sustaining colony born of the quest for oil and strangely at odds with the surrounding primitive country.

To the west, the low blue fingers of the gigantic Andes are visible—here, only 4,000 feet; but as they climb farther westward they soon reach the imposing height of 16,000 feet. To the south, a rolling savanna stretches toward the town of Maturín, capital of the State of Monagas, some 23 miles distant (map, page 100).

It is a country of sharp contrasts, where day descends into the darkness of night without any interlude of twilight.

With the people it is much the same. Wide-eyed little girls bloom into womanhood with a swiftness which ignores adolescence.

There are purple shadows where the mountains meet the sky—shadows that stand like sentinels beyond a row of square frame houses whose peaked red roofs loom up as starkly as tents in the desert. One is sharply aware of utter isolation, yet quite unlonely. For like a living breath comes the sense and the smell of the jungle. The mystery of a thousand unseen living things mingles with the scent of as many flowers, to season the air with magic.

RED-ROOFED HOUSES ON STILTS

To this lotus land I came with my husband, an American oil company representative.

At the top of scarlet hibiscus hedges, our houses are set on 10-foot stilts, high off the ground, to combat the heat. In the space underneath, the family wash blows gaily, free of daily rains (page 102).

Native cooks and nursemaids for the American colony are seen slap-slap-slapping down the sun-baked road in their woven sandals, minus shape or heel. Over their heads they fling a towel to escape the tropic sun; this is replaced by a black veil when they attend Sunday mass.

As servants, they are amusing, but aggravating. They work only when whim dictates, and no bribe of more money will induce dependability. When their mood rebels at work, they invariably come to the door, their arms laden with bright poinsettias, chanting a long lament, "that they are filled with sorrow to leave the good lady for the short space of a day."

Throughout the jungle, which borders us on all sides, lies a constant crisscross of shallow rivers. Here the people of the plains take their baths. Certain hours are reserved in each area for men, and other hours for women. These hours are never violated.

SNAKES SHARE THE SHOWER

Within the camp we have a commissary containing imported canned goods from the United States. Our own chlorinating system safeguards us against the typhoid and dysentery germs that formerly took heavy toll among Venezuelans in this section. As an additional precaution all fresh fruits, vegetables, and eggs must be washed before eating. A company power plant provides electricity and running water for the entire camp. The latest movies arrive by plane twice each week.

It is a strange sort of civilization we enjoy in the midst of this primeval jungle. For, while we escape the steaming heat in our baths, we are not immune to a snake sharing our shower. It never fails to fascinate me that my husband's shoes and our small shower room should prove such a foil for small snakes (page 102). The first time I came upon a mapanare coiled in the corner of the clothes closet, I was so faint with fright that I could only scream feebly for the cook to come and kill it, which she did with amazing nonchalance.

Now, after several years, I have learned

CARACAS HOLDS BRILLIANT STATE RECEPTIONS IN THE FEDERAL PALACE

Guests in gay uniforms and Parisian frocks gather on important holidays beneath the dome of the famous Salon Eliptico. Overhead a stirring fresco by a Venezuelan artist, Tovar y Tovar, recalls the Battle of Carabobo, turning point in the Nation's fight for independence under Simón Bolívar. The palace forms part of the Capitol, built around a garden court (page 131). Government offices are housed in the wing in the foreground.

to detect the slight, almost soundless rustle which precedes a snake's advance. I have learned, too, that scorpions travel in pairs; so, when one is found, we must immediately search for the other. Also, when entering a dark room and immediately turning on the light, I find my eyes riveted in a quick, complete survey of the floor. These and other anticipations become as instinctive as breathing, and nearly as important.

But above and beyond this sense of the sinister is a surface beauty so compelling that it seeps through the senses like a drug. In every varying phase of color, form, and fragrance, this same beauty overshadows the more menacing side of jungle life.

This morning, beside the fragile white orchid swaying under the eaves of my bedroom window, I saw a round black shadow on the screen. It was a tarantula, a terrifying thing with long legs springing from a fat, furred body, and measuring about eight inches in diameter over all. The tarantula was quickly killed and forgotten. The orchid still blooms on—a significant symbol which makes the Tropics a mecca for beauty lovers the world over.

EXCITEMENT OVER AN APPLE

I had supposed, until living down here, that all excitement over an apple died out with Adam; but that was because I had never lived on canned foods for weeks, counting the days until the next boat would bring us fresh vegetables from the States.

Now, when my laundress comes running to the door, shouting: "Madame, madame, apples at the commissary!" I snatch my

Photograph courtesy Grace Line

"TODAY—CIRCUS IS IN TOWN!" SIGNS PROCLAIM

Boys parade through the streets of Caracas with posters announcing the big event. "Great reduction in prices," the placards promise for both afternoon and evening performances.

dark glasses and dash down the sun-baked road with as much fervor as I took to my first circus.

Perhaps half a dozen times a year apples are shipped down from the United States, along with celery, nuts, lettuce, and oranges —big, glowing, golden oranges which put the native fruit of that name to shame. Then, indeed, recklessness runs riot. What would be an ordinary Saturday morning marketing at home assumes the proportions of a jealously guarded gold mine. Incidentally, the transaction also involves plenty of gold. Such delicacies must be eked out for weeks.

GIFTS FROM THE JUNGLE

So, if at any time you should happen to call on a woman in eastern Venezuela and she offers you an apple, be assured you have made a favorable impression.

On the other hand, we have constant gifts from the jungle, which at home are rather rare treats. Heart of palm, for example, grows in the tops of tall, naked trees. The exterior looks like sugar cane. When the outer bark is removed, the tender white stalks make a tempting salad; they provide keen competition for the ever-growing avocado, which peons gather from the forest for one and a half cents each.

Papayas, plentiful as palms, play a proud part in forming the foliage around our house. If eaten at the psychological moment of ripening, these melons add zest to the breakfast hour. Papaya trees must be planted in pairs; without the pollen from the male tree, the female bears no fruit. Mangoes, too, grow profusely throughout the forest; likewise *plátanos* (plantains), the great oversized bananas which are eaten daily by the peon class.

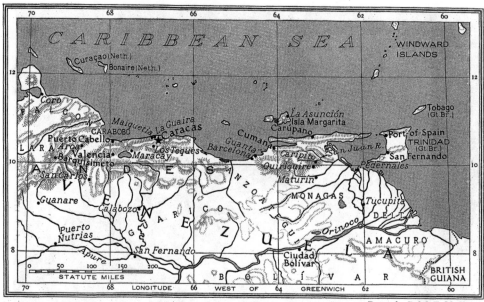

Drawn by Ralph E. McAleer

SPANISH EXPLORERS CALLED THIS CARIBBEAN DIADEM "VENEZUELA"—LITTLE VENICE

Lake dwellings of the Indians reminded them of the old European city of gondolas and canals. Visitors today find little similarity. Modern cities, paved roads, and thriving industries dot the country, yet in the tropical forests primitive life goes on. Deep in the jungle, the author and her husband lived at Quiriquire, a small colony of United States oil representatives. Streams are infested with caymans, snakes abound in water and on land, but above, in the trees, coconuts grow and wild orchids bloom in profusion.

For the rest, the native produce is disappointing. The potato is about the size of a large lime. Lettuce is an inferior type of the leaf variety, better for decorative purposes than for eating. Oranges, as stated, are small, green, and sour. Fresh vegetables, such as peas and string beans, are obtainable only on incoming boats.

BEANS TO CHALLENGE BOSTON

But the beans! Here, indeed, is the Venezuelan staff of life. Red beans, black beans, and white beans come in scores of various flavors and sizes. When soaked overnight and baked for five hours with bacon and jalapeños, a Mexican pepper, the round red beans make a delicious dish. I could really wax eloquent on the subject of beans.

The people of Venezuela reflect the gaiety that is so integral a part of their country. They have the happy hearts of children and a love of life which has proved itself unquenchable.

Along the river's edge the laundresses laugh and sing together as they beat their bright-colored clothes upon the flat stones (page 130). Naked brown babies are merry children of chance, who have no dread of tomorrow as they eat their breadfruit and bananas. And why not! For have they not a hammock which swings them to sleep like a lullaby, a roof of moriche palm, and the fragrance of starflowers to woo them into dreamland?

The tavern is peopled with pink-shirted peons who shout in abandon as they place their bets on the fighting cocks. From the *tiple,* a stringed instrument resembling a ukulele, the strains of *La Cucaracha* spice the soft summer air.

HOSPITALITY OF PLAINS DWELLERS

The plains dwellers never cease to be a source of wonder and delight to me. Their hospitality exceeds anything I have encountered. They are, in a material sense, incredibly poor. They live in one-room mud huts with thatched roof, whose sole furnishing is the hammock in which they sleep. They have never seen a stove, nor even heard about bread and butter. They cook by means of a crude charcoal arrangement in an old iron pot which is upheld by stones. Rice, plátanos, breadfruit, and *casabe* (cassava) form their daily fare.

They have no clothes, except the garment they happen to be wearing at the mo-

Photograph by William Langley

THE AUTHOR MEETS WAYFARERS PREPARED FOR SUDDEN RAINS

As Mrs. Langley poses with the travelers, they keep hood and umbrella ready for action. Caught in a sudden heavy shower, they will be utterly nonchalant. The wet season extends from April to October, but downpours are frequent throughout the dry period.

ment. But they will not let you pass their home without running into the path with some gift. Perhaps it is a bunch of lady-fingers, bananas about three inches long, of a mouth-watering sweetness. It may be a cluster of creamy gardenias which grow luxuriantly in the plains, or again it may be only a great white disk of cassava, the Venezuelan substitute for bread (page 111). Whatever their offering, the spirit which prompts it comes from a friendly heart.

One morning, while riding through the forest, we came upon a scene which caused even my horse to slacken his pace. In a cool grove of tall trees and tangled lianas stood a small thatched hut. Beyond the grove a giant tree sliced the sky, naked save for

the most exquisite orchid plant I have ever seen. There it hung, like a rare jewel, with six or seven enormous white blooms. The sun spilled a thousand splinters of bright white light over the little bamboo hut.

Myriad gleams flirted from the bold brilliance of bougainvillea bushes to the green mango trees which framed the doorway. From a crude charcoal stove the scent of cooking mingled with the heady fragrance of gardenias. The place presented such an inviting air that we were tempted to stop and rest our horses.

No sooner had we dismounted, some twenty feet from the house, than a brown-skinned, calico-clad native woman came running to greet us.

Photograph from Mrs. W. C. Langley

"AIR-CONDITIONING" IN QUIRIQUIRE MEANS 10-FOOT CONCRETE STILTS

The author's red-roofed brick home is cooler and drier in this elevated position than it would be if built on the ground. The "open-air basement" serves a useful purpose—washing dangles gaily there, protected from the daily rains (page 97). Just before a downpour, the author writes, "We are warned by a whispering that blows across the jungle. By the time we have raced through the house to let down the shutters, all the clouds in the heavens have burst their burden."

Photograph by Carlos Ordoniz

LARGEST OF THE BOAS, THE ANACONDA DWELLS IN SWAMPS AND RIVERS

This 22-foot specimen, killed while stealing into the Caripito commissary, is of medium size. Anacondas usually submerge in streams to await animals which come to drink. Like lightning they coil around the prey and crush it. The tough skin is iridescent dark green, with round black spots. Smaller snakes are frequent intruders in Quiriquire homes. Whenever the author entered a room, her first act was to glance hastily about in search of poisonous visitors.

Photograph by William Summers

QUIRIQUIRE BUILDERS ERECT A COOL HOME OF WATTLE AND DAUB

No nails or tools of any sort are required. Nearly all these comfortable dwellings have earthen floors. Sometimes the buildings are whitewashed. Such a mud home rises quickly when rains are frequent.

When we had returned her greeting and begged permission to rest, her enthusiasm was flattering. While she tied our horses, she explained that they were making cassava bread, that they had steaming coffee, and, as an additional incentive, there was a new baby!

THE MAKING OF CASSAVA BREAD

Now, the making of cassava bread had long intrigued me. I had watched it being made in a mill, where all the crude implements were handwork of the miller himself.

But at last we were to see actually practiced at home one of the oldest and most primitive of Venezuelan customs. Inside the hut we found only one large room; each corner held a hammock; and above one of the larger ones, bunk fashion, hung the tiniest hammock I had ever seen. Obviously, the new baby!

Asking if I might look, I pulled back the mosquito netting and was amazed to find a whimpering red baby, as new as the day! "Where is the mother?" asked my friend.

"Graciella, come here and speak with the ladies." The woman beckoned her daughter, who was vigorously peeling the *yuca* root which was to supply the meal for cassava.

"Yes, yes, madame," she murmured, "only this morning, with the sun, came the little one."

"But you!" I protested. "Shouldn't you be resting in the hammock?"

The mother's smile held a hint of condescension, as she proudly replied, "Ah, you Americans, in truth you must lie abed with much pain, and have the doctor. But not my Graciella. For her the making of a baby is so simple as to make bread."

And so it seemed, to our speechless admiration!

On an old piece of tin, through which holes had been punched, Graciella grated the yuca. When this was finished, the pulp was put into a long woven fiber cone, pulled lengthwise to squeeze out the juice (pages 105, 109). During this process two little naked children ran about waving long sticks

Photograph by Loran Kahle

COCONUTS LURE JUAN TO THE TOP OF A TALL PALM TREE

Quiriquire's camp gardener spends much of his time in the treetops, but usually he is gathering orchids, which he sells in the United States colony for one bolívar (32 cents) apiece. He scales the trunk as easily as he would walk upstairs. Orchids, often incorrectly called parasites, are really epiphytes which obtain their moisture and nourishment from the air. While they thrive in profusion high in tropical trees, they do not live at the expense of their arboreal hosts.

Photograph by Loran Kahle

HOMEMADE MACHINERY TRANSFORMS CASSAVA INTO COARSE FLOUR AT A
VILLAGE MILL

Fleshy, cylindrical, tapering roots, sometimes three feet long and filled with milky juice, are cut from cassava plants, plentiful in Venezuelan forests. Here the miller is slicing the tubers to free the fluid, which contains highly poisonous hydrocyanic acid (page 103). To eliminate more of the juice, the roots are grated into a pulp and squeezed in the container hanging from the ceiling. Even then, the dry lumps are still poisonous. Kneaded into large, thin cakes, they are baked thoroughly on a metal plate, and then may be safely eaten.

to frighten away chickens, pigs, and dogs, lest they swallow a drop of the yuca juice, which is poisonous.

The pulp was then removed, shaped into cylinders, and allowed to dry in the sun until brittle enough to break into pieces. These pieces were sifted through a screen to form a meal.

"What seasoning do you use with your meal?" I asked, curiously.

Blank stares from Graciella and her mother.

"This is all."

Dubiously I watched as they patted the meal into large disks, about 28 inches in diameter and thin as a dollar. They then placed these disks on a huge sheet of iron over the coal fire. It was fascinating to watch Graciella flip them as easily as we would a pancake. In place of a cake turner, however, she used only two small sticks, slightly the worse for wear.

In less time than it takes to tell, they turned out a pile of cassava disks, one of which they smilingly offered us.

"It is called the 'sun of Monagas,'" said the old lady. To me, it tasted more like dried-out straw!

THATCHED COTTAGES OF QUIRIQUIRE HUDDLE TOGETHER IN A CLEARING, HEMMED IN BY ENCROACHING JUNGLE

Ceaselessly the inhabitants of this self-sustaining colony in northeastern Venezuela fight off the matted growth. Less than a square mile in area is the settlement, which lies north of Maturín, capital of the State of Monagas (page 97). Scarlet bougainvillea flanks the whitewashed clay walls of the houses and reaches almost to the moriche palm roofs.

Photograph by Joseph Cook

AT THE HEIGHT OF THE RAINY SEASON THE SAN JUAN RIVER GOES ON A RAMPAGE

So low is the ground near Caripito, north of Quiriquire, that the swollen stream spreads for miles across the countryside. Natives in boats are removing all their belongings from the huts, which may be completely submerged. After the waters recede, and the homes dry out, the villagers return.

Photograph by Alfred T. Palmer

CARACAS HONORS HER NATIVE SON, SIMÓN BOLÍVAR

Dominating the Plaza Bolívar, in the heart of the city, rises the memorial statue of the Liberator. Hero of more than 200 battles, this soldier and statesman led the revolutions against Spain that brought independence to Venezuela, Colombia, Ecuador, Panama, Peru, and Bolivia. Caracas claims him as its own, for he was born here about the time the United States gained independence.

of wood as if it were a throne and the plodding burros his faithful subjects. For Jesús is very rich! He comes on not one burro, but two! The one he rides; the other carries two huge baskets dangling on either side like fat, grotesque legs.

One basket contains fresh eggs, wrapped in banana leaves to keep them cool and protect them from breakage. The other contains squawking chickens. Sometimes there is a third basket, with green lemons the size of an orange and deliciously flavored.

Yesterday Jesús swept off his straw sombrero with a flourish:

"For you, madame, I have one inveetayshun . . ."

His liquid black eyes flashed a fire, unusual in their sleepy depths.

However, upon our return home we discovered that, toasted with butter and topped by a bit of plátano that has been baked in cinnamon, it has rather a piquant taste.

EGGS WRAPPED IN BANANA LEAVES

My egg man is a gay caballero named Jesús (pronounced Hay-soos, the most common of all male names in this section of Venezuela). Jesús comes riding through the rain wearing his red poncho as insolently as a toreador. He sits his saddle

"That is nice, Jesús," I answered. "What is the occasion?"

"For ze mos famos of cockfight, madame. Jesús bet mucho dinero, bolívars, one hundred, verdad." Jesús mixes his English and Spanish piquantly.

So at four o'clock my husband and I rode down to the village to watch this sport so beloved of Venezuelans. In front of the shop stood a gala group. Jesús had discarded his poncho for a bright pink shirt.

Upon seeing Bill, he ran forward, thrust

ing his cock high in the air with the eager pride of a child. A jovial bartender hurried forth with a glass of *cocuy* for Bill and red wine for me. Cocuy is a native drink, distilled from the juice of a cactus; it looks as harmless as water, but tastes like nothing so much as liquid fire.

Beyond the store the cockpit ring resembled a miniature football bowl. Benches were arranged in circular tiers. The cockpit itself was approximately ten feet in diameter, with a three-foot circular enclosure. The two fighting cocks looked more grotesque than belligerent. Their wattles and combs had been cut off; their necks and legs were plucked bare. Only a few remaining tail feathers waved triumphantly like a battle flag.

Photograph by Carlos Ordoniz

INDIANS PADDLE HOME WITH MANNA FROM THE WILDERNESS

Guaraunos load their canoe with a cargo of cassava roots cut in the forest. From the tubers they will make their bread. Forest and stream supply nearly all the wants of northeastern Venezuelan tribesmen. Moriche palms furnish thatch and poles for huts, fibers for weaving, and fruit, sap, and pulp for food. Fish and turtles abound in the rivers and game is plentiful in the jungle.

Finally, the fight was on. The two cocks, with spurs tied to their legs, seemed slightly bewildered as to procedure; but after a fierce prodding by their backer, they soon flew at each other with fiendish ferocity.

There is no spirit of compromise in a fighting cock. He wins or dies, in less than five minutes of battle. It is an ugly thing to watch. With a whirring of wings, the two cocks leap into the air and fly at each other like evil spirits. A quick stroke of the spur aimed at a strategic spot in the neck, and it was over, the stricken cock lying in a pool of his own blood.

Bill had placed his bet with Jesús, goading the cock on with lusty cries. Now he reveled in the victory as if it were his own.

I was thankful to see it end. We looked for Jesús to congratulate him; but he was busily squeezing the juice of a lime into the wounds of his victorious cock.

Do you remember, many years ago when your parents took you to charity bazaars, the mysterious curtained-off partition called the "fish pond"? How thrilling it was to throw your pole over the top and breathlessly await the wonders it would yield. It might be a singing top, or a fat little angel carved from white wood. Once, on

EVEN IN QUIRIQUIRE, SATURDAY NIGHT MEANS A BATH!

After a thorough shower, which deluges hair, bracelets, and results in an occasional unwelcome mouthful of water, the little señorita will be ready for her hammock of moriche palm. Ropes, fastening her couch to the roof poles, will squeak a lullaby.

the end of his dangling hook my little brother brought back a fantastic frog that could be wound up and made to hop and croak!

A MAN-EATING FISH

So it is with fishing in the big lagoons. When you toss in your line for a 23-inch bass, you may pull out a man-eating caribe.

That is what happened to us the first time we fished there. Seated in the bottom of our boat, we were trolling with a spoon for bass, when suddenly my husband's line was nearly jerked from his hand. The

sleepy-eyed native at the paddle was instantly alive with excitement.

"Watch out, sir, it is a caribe!"

I was fairly frozen with fear. For the name "caribe" brought back one of the worst experiences we had heard about during our residence in Venezuela (page 123).

A short time ago, a young geologist conducted a party up the Apure River. He halted at the little village of Puerto Nutrias to hire runners. Finding the place utterly deserted, he was about to turn back to his plane when he noticed the town's entire

Photograph by William Langley

STACKED CASSAVA LOAVES RESEMBLE GIANT PANCAKES

Palm leaves protect edges of the pile of thin disks from the binding cord. Ready for delivery, two bundles are hoisted aboard a donkey. One dangles on each side, and the vender perches between. Packets of six sheets are safely transported long distances.

population gathered at the river's edge. He ran down and found a group of excited natives crowding about what must recently have been the body of a woman. Now it was reduced to a bleeding, bony structure from which the flesh had been almost entirely eaten away.

In answer to his questions, he received but one frenzied phrase.

"My God, caribes, caribes!"

Knowing the caribe to be seldom more than 20 inches long, our friend couldn't conceive of one killing an adult. When he said as much, it was explained to him that these cannibal fish travel in schools of a hundred or more; and that at the smell of blood they become menacing and quick as lightning.

It seems that while the woman had been beating her clothes on the stones at the river's edge, she had scratched her hand, causing it to bleed. No sooner had she stepped into the deeper water to rinse her hand, than hundreds of these small fish surrounded her. With vicious bites, they plucked the flesh from her body with the rapidity of flame.

Her first piercing screams brought the

surrounding natives in less than three minutes. But by the time they reached the water's edge she was dead—and the caribes only a dark line in the disappearing stream.

So now, at my look of horror, when our boatmen shouted "Caribe!" Bill hastened to reassure me that there was no danger singly.

After a good bit of fight, they landed him in the boat. The peon slipped his machete in the fish's mouth, while Bill removed the hook. For the caribe has pointed teeth and bites viciously. They say, however, that danger is involved only when the fish smells blood.

A PARADISE FOR BIRD LOVERS

Bird life in eastern Venezuela presents a paradise for ornithologists.* According to a recent guest of ours, Gladys Gordon Fry, the "bird lady" from the American Museum of Natural History, New York, the surrounding jungle offers an unrivaled opportunity for naturalists to spend years of intensive and profitable study.

As yet, this section of Venezuela has been little visited. There are hundreds of specimens which so far have scarcely been touched upon.

Multitudes of parrots and brilliantly plumed macaws brighten the sky like scattered jewels in moving phantasy. From the pet point of view, however, I prefer the troupial, a gay gold-and-black oriole whose lilting song is like a human whistle. So wonderfully clear and musical it sounds that just listening to it lends a lift to one's spirit.

My troupial loves the bright things of life; so we call him "Gem." Anything that shines, even to the raindrops in my hand, Gem pecks at with a vehemence surprising in one of his size. As yet quite young, he is about the size of a catbird, and incredibly tame.

Irrespective of friend or stranger, Gem will perch on any hand that is held out to him. Woe to the fingers that tease him, though, for he will start straight for the owner's eyes with a series of staccato clucks that sound more like those of an angry hen than his usual liquid call.

*See "In Humboldt's Wake" and "Journey by Jungle Rivers to the Home of the Cock-of-the-Rock," by Ernest G. Holt, in the NATIONAL GEOGRAPHIC MAGAZINE, November, 1931, and November, 1933, respectively.

The *oropéndolas* (or great-crested caciques) are also abundant in this section. There is a large colony of them; their hanging nests swing from the branches of a tall tree which faces the gorge in front of our house (page 125).

This flamboyant tree, more than 80 feet in height, flings a shower of brilliant yellow blossoms to the sky like a giant golden goddess. There are two distinct colonies of caciques nesting there, neighbored by wasps' nests for protection!

Hanging from the branches on one side are nine pendent nests of the great-crested caciques; about 40 feet apart, on the branches of the other half of the tree, hang the nests of the yellow-backed caciques.

I was lamenting that I could not obtain a pair of them, when Juan, the camp gardener, broke into smiles: "Yes, yes, madame, them I shall bring to you."

So away he ran, and soon returned carrying a thick rope. Making a long loop of the rope which encompassed the tree trunk as well as his own body, Juan started the slow ascent. Bracing himself against the tree, he took a few flat-footed steps, then gave the rope a quick flip upward and repeated the performance. He was soon up the tree, crawling cautiously out on the branch above the nests. Quickly he detached two of them with his machete, and slid down the tree a great deal more rapidly than he went up.

There was a great fluttering of wings in the air and a series of sharp protesting calls, but Juan dropped safely to the ground with a nest containing three baby oropéndolas. His ankles were slightly the worse for wear.

THE FOOLISH BIRDS

The bird which amuses me most in our jungle is the hoatzin, often called the "foolish bird," and known as the missing link between the bird and animal kingdom. The young hoatzin has prehistoric hands with claws on the "fingers." These birds hover so awkwardly in flying that one wonders why they were equipped with wings.

Among nocturnal birds—and there are many—the guacharos and owls seem the noisiest. The guacharo is distant cousin to the whippoorwill which calls in summer from northern woods. Although the body is like a nighthawk, its weird, disklike eyes are decidedly owlish. From the depths of the jungle the guacharo comes to perch in

Photograph by Hanns Tschira from European

CATHEDRAL-LIKE CARACAS UNIVERSITY IS SIX YEARS OLDER THAN HARVARD

Spanish priests founded the institution as a theological seminary in 1630. A petition for its establishment had been signed nearly forty years before that. Here in Venezuela's capital, where old and new mingle, horse-drawn vehicles still compete with automobiles.

LA GUAIRA, SEAPORT FOR CARACAS, SNUGGLES AT THE FOOT OF THE EASTERN ANDES

Open to the sea is the harbor, where a merchantman rides at a mooring. Almost always a heavy ground swell rolls in, on which bob ships' boats bound for shore. Behind the town a concrete highway to Caracas winds up the slopes (pages 116 and 126). High on the mountainside stands the old Spanish fort that once protected the town. Today it is merely a signal station for ships.

Photograph from Pix

SUBURBAN DWELLERS DRIVE TO CARACAS OVER MOHEDANO BRIDGE, ON A SUPER HIGHWAY

This modern span is named for the Spanish priest who first brought the coffee plant to Venezuela from Martinique in 1784. Today coffee is the Nation's foremost crop. The bridge lies between the city and newly developed areas dotted with palatial villages. Near by is Los Caobos Avenue (page 132), named for the long rows of mahogany trees that flank it on each side.

Photograph by Ernest G. Holt

SERPENTINE ROADS WITH HAIRPIN CURVES LINK CARACAS AND THE SEA

Motor highway and railroad zigzag sharply up the steep sides of a rocky gorge, twisting 23 miles between the port of La Guaira and the capital. As the crow flies, the distance between the two cities is less than seven miles (pages 114 and 126). Here, from the vantage point of Mora's Rock, most of narrow Tacagua Valley is revealed, with the railroad bridge far below spanning the river bed, dry in summer months.

Photograph from Publishers' Photo Service

IN VENEZUELA'S "WESTMINSTER," THE PANTHEON, REST HER NATIONAL HEROES

Simón Bolívar's ashes are at the foot of a marble memorial to the Liberator, in the center of the cathedral-like structure. His heart is buried at Santa Marta, Colombia, where he died. Surmounting his tomb is a statue of South America's "George Washington," carved by Tenerani, Italian sculptor. Other notables are buried near by. The building, facing on the Plaza Miranda, originally was designed and built as a church (page 131).

AT THE FOOT OF MASSIVE MOUNT AVILA, CARACAS SPRAWLS ACROSS A PLATEAU 3,025 FEET ABOVE THE SEA

Spires and steeples of the capital's many churches rise above red-tiled roofs. In the northwestern section of the city (left), La Pastora Church stands on an eminence. At right, where garden-covered Calvary Hill begins its ascent, Calvary Chapel overlooks busy streets. The large white building (center) is the new home of the Ministry of Education, not yet completed, and to its right the round tower of the Cathedral looms above Plaza Bolívar. White villas fleck the landscape in the background.

Photograph by Philip D. Gendreau

DERRICKS RISE ABOVE THE PALMS, BOOM TOWNS MUSHROOM AT THEIR FEET, IN THE BASIN OF LAKE MARACAIBO

Tall towers dot the Santa María landscape, driving water boas and caymans from their haunts. Throughout northwestern Venezuela oil is king. The port of Maracaibo, headquarters of many operating companies, has grown in a few years from a jungle town to a thriving city, exporting nearly 150,000,000 barrels of oil annually.

HERE VENEZUELA'S LAWMAKERS MEET IN CARACAS

The columned façade graces the south face of the Capitol, with legislative halls for Chamber of Deputies and Senate. Relic of old colonial days is the centuries-old ceiba (silk cotton) tree. Within the shade of its boughs, at San Francisco Place in the background, stockbrokers gather on weekdays at a curb market, chief financial exchange of the country.

Photographs by Ernest G. Holt

GRACEFUL ARCHES LEAD TO THE PATIO OF THE CAPITOL AND PALACE

These all-purpose government buildings, occupying a whole city square, surround a garden. Through the archway, and across the street, a modern building houses shops.

our papaya trees and screech in constant competition with the yodeling toucan.

The most prolific of our bird colonies are the lovely little puff birds, which build in the sandbanks and gladden the still summer air with a soft sweet song. The "God birds," as the peons call wrens, do their daily duty in awakening us each morning.

THE BELLBIRDS' SILLY SYMPHONY

But the most whimsical of all, both in song and movement, are the bellbirds. They flit about in the branches of our spreading ceiba trees in a manner that would endear them to Walt Disney for his Silly Symphonies. They are about the size of a large robin, but so elusive I have never been able to get close enough to see whether they are brown or black. They call "dong-rong, dong-rong" with the metallic clarity of a silver bell.

They always seem to fly in pairs. When one calls, the other answers, so there is a duality of song, which on a clear day may be heard over a mile away.

A BUSHMASTER IN CAMP

No one warned me two years ago that I would ever run for a month-old newspaper with the avidity of a child after candy. But that was long before I had learned to depend upon the radio for my one contact with the outside world.

News in Quiriquire takes two forms— that which we receive by radio, bringing us flashes from a world of action, and that other form of "news" which has to do with daily life in the jungle. The latter lends constant color to what might otherwise prove a monotonous existence.

Scarcely an hour ago Bill rushed in with the news that a 7-foot bushmaster had just been killed in front of the labor office. We lost no time in loading our camera and dashing down to catch a picture of it, still warm and half-coiled.

Although mapanares, fer-de-lance, and boas are common enough in this part of Venezuela, during two years we have seen but three bushmasters killed in our forest.

While we are on the subject, I must tell a most dramatic snake story. The event occurred during a trip down the Orinoco Delta upon which I accompanied my husband. It is a thrilling tale of a vicious water battle between a cayman and a water boa, or anaconda; so unusual was it, not

only to me, during my three years' stay in the country, but to our Venezuelan neighbors, that had we not taken photographs for proof, I shouldn't blame anyone for raising an eyebrow in skepticism.

Taking the Stanocoven launch from Caripito wharf, we soon left the San Juan and entered one of the many branches of the Orinoco.

Along this stream there is much to gladden the eye. Snow-white egrets wing their way in colorful contrast with scarlet ibis. Red howler monkeys swing themselves by their tails from tree to tree, bruising the soft summer air with savage screams.* Orchids bloom in profusion from many derelict treetops.

INDIANS WADE IN RIVER TO CATCH THEIR DAILY MEAL

Dotting the gunmetal waters of the mighty river are occasional clusters of squat, potbellied Indians wading out from shore to catch their daily meal of fish. Drifting past hillside pueblos of abandoned charm, we finally reached our destination on the Orinoco Delta, the houseboat of an American oil company. It was piloted by Stanley Simmons, a young geophysical prospector.

With a crew of twenty natives he worked up and down the side streams, searching the creepy, matted undergrowth for oil structures.

Simmons had penetrated places where no white man had ever entered. He had cut his way through the tangled jungle with a machete. He had thirsted in the jungle until his sole source of water was to slash a slender stalk of vine.

For five years his only home had been this dilapidated houseboat which his native crew had named the *Ark*. When we pulled up beside his boat, his pleasure at seeing us was significant of a man who has too long been deprived of speaking his own language.

From the deck of the *Ark* we watched a kaleidoscopic scene flash from the banks of the river. Beauty runs rampant along the Orinoco. Proud palms spike the sky with gay green blades. From the luxuriant undergrowth of the jungle flame thousands of tropical flowers. Our eyes followed a group of macaws, flying ever in pairs, scattering their brilliant plumage like miniature

*See "Monkey Folk," by William M. Mann, NATIONAL GEOGRAPHIC MAGAZINE, May, 1938.

FOR HIS PORTRAIT, JESÚS DONS A PINK
SHIRT!

With ever-present machete he slashes his way
through the jungle. Every native carries one of
the big broad knives, manufactured in Connecticut.

rainbows amid the dazzling tropic sunshine.

I envied the bright birds their facility
of movement, wishing I could transport
myself back, for a brief instant, to a land
where skyscrapers break the sky line with
brittle modernity. But suddenly I was
startled out of my dreaming by a native
crying, "Snake, snake!"

We all sprang forward to look. There,
in the center of some matted vegetation,
lay an enormous water boa enjoying a full-
bellied siesta. It was immediately evident
that this was no ordinary boa. For there
was a big bulge, extending about seven feet
through his stomach, outmeasuring the
snake many times in diameter. Because
of the boa's semidormant condition after
eating, it was but a matter of moments
before a peon with a few swift strokes of
his machete severed his head and life.

SNAKE SWALLOWS CAYMAN

Now, snakes are common enough to Simmons and his crew. But they instantly
realized that here was something most
extraordinary. So they tied the big, bulg-
ing boa to the back of the boat and towed
him to the nearest encampment, about 18
miles downstream. There they stretched
him out on the bottom of a small fishing
boat. He measured approximately 19 feet
in length.

Then Simmons, breathless with curiosity
as to the nature of that bulge, slit the
snake's stomach and disclosed the slightly
decomposed body of a 6-foot cayman.

What a jungle battle that must have
been! There, upon one among hundreds
of floating islands which dot that lovely,
lonely stretch of water, ensued a struggle
to thrill even Frank Buck.

To us laymen, the mystery remains that
a snake whose mouth measured not more
than three inches in diameter could have
swallowed a crocodilian whose body measured more than ten inches in diameter, not-
withstanding the fact that a snake's mouth
can stretch incredibly.

Furthermore, what was the cayman do-
ing to permit himself to be swallowed
headfirst? For caymans can deal a death
blow with their tails. That the snake took
some punishment was evident from the
marred condition of its skin. But how it
ever escaped this Orinoco bully is just another jungle mystery. The most likely
explanation is that the snake found the
cayman asleep on the matted vegetation,

Photograph by Charles Jackson

DEADLY IS THE STRIKE OF THE CARIBE, FRENZIED AT THE SMELL OF BLOOD

Traveling in schools of a hundred or more in South America's tropical streams, these fish are capable of reducing human beings to a skeleton in a few minutes (page 110). A drop of blood from a cut suffered by a bather, laundress, or fisherman attracts them instantly. When they charge *en masse* the water is lashed into a whirlpool as they voraciously swallow every shred of flesh.

Photograph by Thomas F. Lee

LUSTY BRAYS HERALD THE PRESENCE OF THE CARACAS BAKER BOY

As he delivers bread and rolls to a housewife, the burro expresses vocal resentment at the wait. Between the containers, atop the animal's back, the deliveryman rides from house to house.

WHAT DID THIS BIG BOA SWALLOW, TO BULGE ITS BELLY SO?

Semidormant after a jungle battle, the 19-foot anaconda was enjoying a siesta on a lonely island in the Orinoco Delta. A native discovered and killed it (page 122).

Photographs by Stanley Simmons

SLIT OPEN, THE WATER BOA REVEALS A 6-FOOT ALLIGATOR

The snake's mouth, measuring not more than three inches across, had expanded enormously to admit a cayman ten inches in diameter. Slowly and painstakingly it had swallowed its victim headforemost. The author believes the snake coiled itself around the alligator while it slept.

and, fastening his coils around him, crushed him before he fully regained consciousness.

Leaving the snake at Pedernales, we pushed on up Delta Amacuro, where we came upon the remnants of a camp of Guarauno Indians (page 109). The deserted huts along the river bank were eloquent evidence of a late tragedy. We turned the boat toward the shore and came upon the last rites of an Indian burial.

INDIANS' SURFACE CEMETERIES

Following the Guarauno custom, each member of the tribe is buried in his own boat, called a *cayuco*. The body is first covered with mud, leaving the feet exposed, and wrapped tightly in palm leaves. The cayuco is then lifted high in the air, supported by two stout poles which are planted firmly in the ground.

The Guaraunos are an ingenious race, living in palm-roofed huts along the banks of the Orinoco. From the swampland they extract rubber, gold, and tannic acid, which they exchange for food and clothes.

Photograph by Oswald Latrobe

BREEZES ROCK YOUNG CACIQUES IN THEIR PENDULOUS NESTS

From the branches of a tall tree, which faces a gorge in front of the author's house, dangle the homes of two colonies. Usually they build close to wasps' nests for protection against predatory prowlers. Some of the shelters belong to great-crested caciques; others to their yellow-backed cousins, both of which are related to the North American orioles (page 112).

Returning to the boat, we watched the night fall suddenly. A vague nostalgia crept over me for the sun-drenched twilights of Washington. But, as if in answer to a nameless wish, there came an alien rushing sound in the waters; and with one accord the men caught their searchlights and spears.

Following the light cast by Bill's flashlight, I looked into what seemed dozens of bright bits of glass on the surface of the water. Then, with the aid of half a dozen lamps playing about, I saw them—scores of caymans churning the water in angry protest.

Spearing them was amazingly quick

STEEPLY RISES THE ROAD TO CARACAS AS CARIBBEAN AND LA GUAIRA FADE INTO THE DISTANCE

Through the little fishing village of Maiquetía, the highway ascends from the capital's seaport (background). Tall cacti, simulating sentinels, rise from the slopes on either side. Originally built by the Spaniards, the road was widened and paved as a motor highway about fifteen years ago. It was the forerunner of Venezuela's network of modern roads, one of which stretches from Caracas to the Colombian border and beyond (page 116).

Photographs by Loran Kahle

"I KNOW THEY'RE GOOD—I SAMPLED 'EM"

The happy pastry and candy vender is one of a large army of boys who stroll through the cities and pueblos of Venezuela, carrying their sweets on wooden trays. Often the delicacies are made by their mothers.

HOLLYWOOD STARS MIGHT TRY THIS TO GAIN POISE!

Screen actresses ruefully balance books on their heads to acquire the graceful carriage that everyday chores give to the Venezuelan water girl. Household tasks begin in childhood.

Photograph by Philip Andrews

AT A SQUARE TURN ON A MOUNTAIN HIGHWAY STANDS A MONUMENTAL WRECK

Motorists, speeding along the serpentine road that leads from La Guaira to Venezuela's gay capital of Caracas, pass this grim warning halfway to the top (pages 126 and 130). On its pedestal is an inscription, "Slowly One Goes Far." Broken guardrails elsewhere along the route give evidence that all do not heed the warning.

Photograph by Loran Kahle

THIS VENEZUELAN DAVID ADDS A GAS-PIPE BARREL TO HIS SLINGSHOT

In the savanna country, where rifles are an expensive luxury, substitutes are invented. Stock and trigger are of wood. Twisted rubber bands, suddenly released, hurl pebble "bullets" with surprising force and speed at birds and small game.

Photograph from Pix

LINK OF FRIENDSHIP IS THE LIBERATOR BRIDGE BETWEEN VENEZUELA AND
COLOMBIA

Spanning the Tachira River in the southwestern corner of Venezuela, this suspension span is
named for Bolívar (pages 108 and 131). It is part of the motor thoroughfare that stretches nearly
800 miles from Caracas to Cúcuta, Colombia. This unit in the Trans-Andean Highway passes
through San Cristóbal and cuts across the Andes at an altitude of 14,000 feet.

work. Only two out of the group were
caught. Now their skins are dried and
rolled in salt to be carried to the States and
there be made into sport shoes and hand-
bags.

FLYING TO CARACAS

From where we live, Caracas is a thrilling
trip by air; flying up, up over the coastal
range of the Andes, we looked down on
slope after slope of brilliant green mountains.

There are no ribboned highways to
whiten the surface of the earth, only a network of ever-interlacing rivers that look
like so many twisting snakes. Higher and
still higher we flew, until the coastal spur
of the Andes resembled the wrinkled face
of an old crone who squinted her eyes
against the bright, white light of fleecy
clouds.

So the plane climbed up the green stair-
steps that followed peak upon peak until
suddenly we swooped down between two
tall peaks to glide out over the island-
studded waters that form a pretty prelude
to Guanta's harbor.

Guanta is like a Gauguin canvas. It is
a pueblo by the sea—and such a sea!
Water with the true blue clarity of a
sapphire turns to clearest emerald along
the shore line. Cool groves of coconut
trees along the water's edge shadow whitewashed adobe huts. A Venezuelan gunboat
lay at anchor. From somewhere on deck
a tiple made merry Spanish tunes.

Dozens of men carrying coal on their
heads kept step to the music as they
mounted the long gangplank. Children
driving their goats along the water's edge
stopped to smile as we clapped our hands
to the music.

To the right of the harbor loomed the
island of Margarita, famous for pearl fish-

Photograph by William Langley

CLOTHESPIN MERCHANTS WOULD STARVE IN QUIRIQUIRE

At the river's edge the laundress lustily pounds her washing upon flat stones, then spreads the clothes along the bank to dry. Three or four good washday sessions bleach a pair of khaki trousers as white as bed linen. Buttons suffer severely.

eries. When the plane shrilled the "all aboard" signal, I was sorry to leave Guanta.

The last stop was La Guaira, landing port for Caracas (page 114). From there we went by motor to the gay capital city; and I am willing to wager that even climbing the Alps holds no more palpitations than that ride up and down the mountain.

Near the modern concrete highway runs one of the most picturesque mountain railways in the world. It connects La Guaira, the chief port of Venezuela, with Caracas, the capital. The distance between the two cities, in a straight line, is less than 7 miles; but the road twists in and out over the mountains, covering about 23 miles.

GRIM REMINDERS TO MOTORISTS

Like a spiral staircase, the road winds up, up, and up, until one fairly feels the sky. Cars whiz by like rockets, careening around curves in a glad, mad rush to reach the gayest of Venezuelan cities. On one side the mountain rises abruptly; the other is sheer nothing—a drop of some 2,000 feet to level land (pages 116 and 126).

Halfway to the top an effigy hints a warning to reckless drivers. It is a demolished car that had been salvaged after it had hurled its occupants over the mountain.

There are other warnings. At intermittent places along the road we noticed blank spots in the guardrail—mute evidence of other catastrophes (page 128). But even these grim reminders failed to dim our eager anticipation of the city.

At the summit we stopped for coffee and looked down on a colorful panorama spread out hundreds of feet below. Then off again! Circling down, down, and down,

Photograph courtesy Grace Line

ROYAL PALMS TOWER OVER RED TILE ROOFS OF THE CARACAS COUNTRY CLUB

Formal gardens, an 18-hole golf course, and a swimming pool fed by springs on the club grounds
surround this social center. Caracas also maintains four other country clubs.

we finally reached the red-roofed city that
is the pride of all Venezuelans (pages 98,
99, 113, 115, 118, 120, 123).

A CITY OF CONTRASTS

Narrow winding streets invested the en-
trance with the aspect of Montmartre.
Here again, what contrasts! Modern structures stand beside adobe houses that look
as if they began with time. Cars, as thick
as trees in the jungle, represent the finest
of American and foreign makes. At an
intersection the line of luxurious motors
halted, and, like a pause from a past cen-
tury, two lazy oxen meandered across the
street pulling a cart piled high with sugar
cane. The peon who drove them held an
old iron cowbell in his hand, which he
tinkled as proudly as his neighbor sounded
the horn of his Packard.

Down in the heart of the city, like a

lovely surprise, we came upon Plaza Bolívar. It is a great sunken square with
spreading ceibas whose cool shadows are
like a benediction to passing people.

Although there is a conventional, and
quite splendid, statue of Bolívar in the center of the square, Plaza Bolívar is decidedly
not just another city park (p. 108). It em-
bodies a natural beauty as untouched by
civilization as a remote corner of the jungle.
In the four corners orchids bloom from
the treetops. Little boys with wood trays
strapped over their shoulders stroll through
the park selling lollipops and fruit (p. 127).

Other shrines where the memory of the
Liberator is honored are the duplicate of
the home in which he was born, which
houses an art gallery and museum, and his
tomb, beneath the cupola of the Pantheon,
Venezuela's Westminster Abbey (p. 117).

Facing the plaza are the most modern

shops, sandwiched in between buildings that look as if they might date from the Conquistadores. Lottery venders besiege every passer-by, flinging promised riches in the air with their long paper banners. Old women, wearing short black mantillas, squat on the sidewalk with trays of wares that boast everything from rosaries and sparkling bits of costume jewelry to pictures of favorite saints.

No one hurries through the streets. The leisurely manner of movement characterizes Caracas as truly Latin.

This city of 248,000 souls was founded by Diego de Losada in 1567. It remained under Spanish rule until the revolt under its native son, Simón Bolívar, when independence was established at the Battle of Carabobo in 1821.

ALONG MAHOGANY DRIVE

Driving from the heart of the city, one passes through Avenida de Los Caobos, known among the English-speaking colony as Mahogany Drive. It is a long arched driveway of mahogany trees bordered by gardens of indescribable beauty. Coming from the blinding glare of a Caracas noonday sun, its shadowed shelter lends a cool cloak of charm to carry you from the city.

Once again, the contrasts, so characteristic of Venezuela, are sharply drawn in the picture presented by the Caracas Country Club (page 131). The interior is enhanced by fine mosaic floors and exquisite wrought-iron grillwork. There you find the epitome of skilled architecture; but in the surrounding grounds you catch your breath at a beauty that speaks of God's work rather than man's.

Every bit of natural beauty has been skillfully utilized. Majestic jungle trees stand in careless clusters, a triumph over the artifice of having been planted by man.

Looking beyond the club one sees a silvery waterfall cascading between two tall peaks of the lower mountain range. That foamy veil of water, so fragile in appearance as to seem only decorative, is in reality the sole source of water supply of the entire community.

Going back through the city, we passed Government House, a cream-colored, sprawling Spanish building with enormous inner courts and gardens. Then we turned in to El Paraíso, the hibiscus-bordered winding avenue that boasts many of the

most imposing residences of the old Caraqueños. It extends along the low hills on the immediate outskirts of the city, topped by an arch of spreading chaparro trees.

All of the houses on El Paraíso have names which seem to have been acquired through some sentimental source, such as the favorite daughter of the house, a significant flower, or even a fancied phrase. They are melodious names, in perfect harmony with this mellowed avenue. Quinta Azul, Las Carretas, Villa Themis, La Parra, and many more, equally inviting, add to the zest of an invitation within their proud portals.

A book could be written on the churches of Caracas. As in Paris, nearly every third or fourth street corner holds one. They are beautiful buildings, the stained-glass windows and statuary of which frequently vie with those in some of the cathedrals of old Europe. From an architectural standpoint, the University also is interesting.

We who came from the jungle were filled with wonder at Club La Suiza, where one is transported in the whisk of an eyelash to the sophistication of New York. It boasts a cosmopolitan crowd and a Cuban rumba band that renders American swing music incomparably!

THE CHARM OF MODERN CARACAS IN CONTRAST TO THE LURE OF THE JUNGLE

But it is not in Caracas that I would paint my picture of Venezuela. For us it held the momentary magic of a good cinema —watching jai alai in the annex of the Club La Suiza, dancing on the roof of the Madrid where the floor felt like glass under our feet, eating hayacas (similar to tamales, but several times as large) at the home of a Venezuelan friend, and finishing dinner with Fundador (a fine Spanish brandy) in our coffee.

All that was but a brief glimpse into an orbit of civilization which stands apart from the Venezuela which we have learned to know and to love.

So I would take you back to our jungle for your last look. Back, where our night life is embodied in the Southern Cross above whispering palms. I would take you back to a sky whose brilliance is strange and awesome to northern eyes—back to a land where a thousand small sounds, seeping through the jungle, mingle with the fragrance of as many flowers to lure you into dreams.

CPSIA information can be obtained
at www.ICGtesting.com
Printed in the USA
BVHW09s1957131018
530034BV00002B/247/P